sissy moral universe

poems by
Christopher Yeates

Of these poems, "Strangers" appeared in *Interim* 1998. The author wishes to thank
the editors of this publication.

ISBN: 978-0-6152-0332-4

Images:
"mother earth" © 2008 by Natalie Woodward, pg. 12
"city of angels" © gobotoru – Fotolia.com, pg. 82
"different" © by Vadim Rybakov - Fotolia.com, cover
"around the world" © by Vadim Rybakov - Fotolia.com, back cover
"maillot beauté" © emilie froquet – Fotolia.com, pg. 106
"the other side" © gobotoru – Fotolia.com, pg. 28

This book is dedicated to my friends and family, to those who believed in me while I believed in nothing, to those who held me up even as I struggled thoughtlessly to fling myself towards rock bottom, to those who have so generously been my spine ever since it was stolen.

And this book is dedicated to my Uncle Bill.

Contents

angels with stolen halos

a brutal and sexy oscillation

epilogue

"Writers are abusive little alchemists. Somewhere in their veins, amidst the abuse of boluses, booze, coffee beans and nicotine, brews a ferocious yet timid megalomania that compels the blood to surrender entirely to its freshly distilled heart.

And then, with the chemical muse in mind, does the writer at last hope to compose the singular, the synthetic, and sometimes even the sublime."

Prologue

If I had someone
To throw my head into tonight,
To toss it like a bowling ball
In their lap,
Weighing the pounds of self-pity,
Staring at their eyes –

I would cry. For things that have been,
And things that are not, and for things
As they are
In this, my land of racing snails
And severed puppy-dog tails.

lucid dreams of deer meat and caviar

Salt Lake City, July 16th

Our feet like paper snowflakes
Drifted in foreign waters.

It was Switzerland then
And home meant nothing.
We stole beer, if you remember.
It was a silly thing to steal.
And we loved Switzerland for
Never catching us.

Home was vacant.
The world was lusted for.
It was Switzerland then,
Switzerland forever.

Inspiration

A young girl with her hair shaped like an altocumulus cloud thinks lazily about writing something. Her friends all tell her to shape up, but she insists she's already round enough. No one understands. When they begin to prod her with pig poles, the head of every Andy Warhol gets stuck beneath her skin.

He paints portraits of Campbell soup cans on the linings of her stomach. She feels elated yet with scissors decides to cut herself into snowflakes and fall throughout the pangs of poets everywhere.

Date

I saw the twenty-six year-old infant drowning in that sweet sea of anxiety.

And told my lover, "How about that."

She was picking lice from my pubic hair. "Should we do something?" I thought about this, but watching her gentle hands scour through the hairs of my frail naked body – I couldn't muster a single concern.

"Of course not," I said. "If we save the manchildren, what will the plankton eat?"

Neuchatel, Juillet 12th

I was a sun child. And a gypsy.
Maybe a vagabond. Also a liar.
I could never decide on a vocation,
let alone a geneology. No.
My time is spent sourly thinking
of sorrows; but the coffee pot is warm,
and the whiskey packs its punch.

When I came upon that small child
bathing herself in sewer water
I was so disgusted that I
held her hand, and we danced
until the sun came to eat us.

I think toute le mond and believe
it is a sissy moral universe.

Recreation

The slender boy near the back of the bar stood up and began talking about serotonin. The only thing listening was a rain cloud, and even it was well on its way to the Pacific.

"They are messing with my mind, with my medications," said the boy. He then grew three times his size, sighed, and suddenly collapsed with enough force to create a new universe.

The things beyond – you know, the blitherblather and the jabberwock – they wondered why they'd never made it to the ark. Ceasing to exist, they couldn't protest the proverbial apocalypse.

But unnamed planets and particles danced a different creation. Brand new eons heard the echo of self-pity.

And somewhere in a pool of proteins, the first pale ale was born.

The New Year

We bypassed time, and stood on a train track
laughing with pints in hand at the forthcoming fireworks;

like a bent quarter we lay gazing at the stars, feeling
the rumble of death in our bones, the not quite silent,
adolescent cry of a desperate, racing, reckless,
bound and childish choo-choo.

We grew bored, grew indebted to debt relief.
We graze with our mowers, chew our coffee,
and laugh idly at political cartoons.

Did you know Leonard killed himself Thursday?
He was twenty-six.
He left a note; it read, "Get real, you bastards."

Nobody knows what the fuck it meant.

Every Sea

About the scourge of human affairs, there is little to say. One voice might spark up and speak, "Thou art ignorant, all mortals." But the cartoons are hit by rubber anvils dangling harmlessly from existential parachutes. Everything bumbles around aimlessly with very real stars encircling their heads, each wondering why great thoughts must sound like Shakespeare.

And Shakespeare himself picks his nose, examines his crisp boogers, and swallows with great shame the harrowing pride of the elite.

Praha, August 12th

The residue of stress softly
like a bag lady,
like a domino,
like a razor smiling at your wrist,
drips onto dead men;

a very European cemetery
sprawls out before you.

The books say nothing, at
least nothing about
the thin courage that is snitching,
the waffling justice of stealing,
the old stones,
the Communists, the concrete –
the residue sloshes against
the throat of a statue, and the statue,
well,
he swallows Listerine even
despite the thin instructions
on the bottle.

Taboo

Everyone welcomes the world at twenty-six. The metabolism is slowing, wrinkles like wallpaper peeling are stretching silently across the faces of everyone. The beer is cold. The brain is throbbing. The heart is throbbing. Everything is growing empty and throbbing.

Meanwhile, the shelves are lined with self-help books. Everyone has advice. The world like a hot air balloon expands with optimism and Joe-Blow says that word processors stand in the way of women.

And it works. The wolves howl at the moon for attention. The world closing its eyes is pretending to wink.

Perversions

Tom isn't peeping anymore and Peter
won't crawl under desks to look up
ladies' dresses. Michael sees a psychiatrist.
Stuart took a vow of celibacy and Greg
proposed at eighteen. He spends all day
in his bathroom beating himself, pacing
his orgasm to meet an imaginary her.
Brett used to hide in the bushes with binoculars.
I took a camcorder and when our parents
were sleeping on secretlonelyboy nights
we'd watch the tapes in cryptic awe
uneasily rubbing ourselves in the pocket of our pants.

All that stark naked serenity –
she and her silhouette were ephemeral
in the window while we were young.

I wear her trash-stained underwear and feel
as if I might bellydance my way through puberty,
making love to everyone alone again.

Acescent

The clown without a rubber nose is walking down the wall.

"Friendship is like all great lies religious by nature," he preaches. "Friends are dogma. Friends are bullshit. Friends are bile. Friends will call their criticism sarcasm, and their animosity good humor." He pauses briefly to juggle a baby and give birth to a couple kitchen knives. "Everyone hides behind the shadow of comedy. The great applause of laughter is nothing but the regret of childhood, the resentment of growing old, the cold vacuous gasp of nostalgia quickly forgotten."

But Jeremy and James and John and Joe are all circle-jerking in the middle of a snowstorm. Sally and Susie and Stacey are busy tying nooses instead of braids. The sexes can't agree.

"You hide behind alliterations," screeches the clown, "and would just as soon stab each other in the back as drop a quarter at the penny arcade."

Afterliving

A fat man with forty-pound jowls is peeling his blubber off in sheets. He fashions them together as a flag, which he then protests quickly by burning. He notes, "There is a thin line between self-deception and self-loathing, but not as thin as the line between sadness and spite."

A small angel taught him to sew. He crushed her between his fingers at her request. Like everything ethereal, she grew tired of eternity. Even God is requesting euthanasia, but the fat man trying to sew his six-hundred and thirty-seventh flag demands a new needle and thread.

"Nietzsche is waiting," God is wailing.

"You sad bastard. You try sewing these flags with a needle as dull as a bone."

Praha, August 23rd

Sometimes you can taste
the two-dimensional sensual
razor in your mouth,
the metallic taste of loneliness.

Gratitude is deep red,
blood red,
like a herring.

Fed

In the midway you can win megalomaniacs if you simply toss three rings atop a bottle. The town drunk has been trying for hours now. Christine Sue pulls at his pant leg.

"They're not always fun," she says to him. "They're a lot of responsibility."

She tells the man about her father. He sweats grease, which they use to fry potato skins. "You know what the secret is?" she says. "You have to feed him ego all day long."

The town drunk passes out and envisions a megalomaniacal train, where the hopeful feed neither cinders nor coal to the engine but instead shovel pure ego into his fat steam face.

The drunk giggles in his sleep. The steam-engine face is merely mechanical. The way it opens and closes like a nutcracker, cracking and swallowing and gnawing at every piece of charred-ego-gristle.

The town drunk awakes and tells Christine Sue he knew a man just like that. "The Don Quixote of nobodies," he said. "He'd take naps in the self-help aisle of book stores, and surrounded himself with only those who would shovel that gristle into his mouth."

"What ever happened to him?"

"He tricked his sadness into thinking it was happiness, and traded his integrity for a toothpick."

And together they shared a bag of potato skins.

sissy moral universe

Praha, August 10th

The door isn't knocking
And neither is the absence welcome

It just sits, stubborn
Like a fat mule in mud, like
A haystack missing its needle

You open it and ask
Politely the absence to move on
You roll around naked in the hallway
You remember things you don't remember
You hinge yourself to a room
Where a lonely old mustached man sits
Whispering in his whiskey
And cackling you sprawl out and
Knock yourself, over and over again

A Genuine Whatever

she
means more than
a red wheelbarrow
glazed by white chickens
in the rain
or whatever

because you can't trust even
the poetry anymore
to be genuine or sententious

no
it's terse it's sad it's
unlike her
and yet like her
it requires not a leap
but swift rape of faith

Spiral

It is a warm evening when
you realize that her arms
draped over you like
wrinkled basilisks are
pressing more than
her body weight.

You are watching girls swoon,
spinning mini-skirts, freshly smooth
seventeen year-old legs
spiraling on the dance floor.

Your father has diabetes;
your mother does too.

In a kind of broken speech
you say something about
castinets and age;
it is the first thing you've said
since the moon stole your smile,
since your childhood usurped
your mind, the tos and fros of
sticks and stones, your own ouroboros
happily digesting the sweet
and sour of your soul.

In the morning the bitter taste
of an evening spent stalled,
aged, and shoving the brush
inside your mouth you scrape
away that accrued holistic decay,
preparing to smile once and forever
again.

broken bird

broken bird in the breezeway of academic halls,
i passed you passing by after i had said goodbye
to Professor Paul, the ardor of my continental youth

i stepped into the world wondering why and how
or perhaps Kant had called to you, broken bird?
did he will that the worms should snatch like a rubberband
you from the grass? or did he will that worm-feeding is
god-awful, that categorically you should starve
broken bird in the breezeway of these, our concrete halls?

four years now with Professor Paul and philosophy,
the continental starving at the expense of careers
i thought about your breast, broken bird, about your
cock-eyed bounces and nervous twitches, about how
you did not flee from me passing through or passing by
after having said goodbye you did not flee from the hollow
analytic academia of Orson Spencer Hall

perhaps that wondering outside world
with its rice and shoelaces and celluloid love –
yes, perhaps, you prefer the tomb, the breezes
sacrificing all that is baffling and beautiful
for the passing through and by and death
stuck,
broken bird in the breezeway of academic halls

Neuchatel, Juillet 17th

does what it mean to be a problem at heart?
an old lush scratching his epitaph on a tombstone
I keep throwing gum to the pigeons
In a coffee house a black man dances
and sweats beads of pure joy; I ramble on and about
berets breasts Bethanies

what a lush! au revoir dead pigeons,
on my way to hug a black man,
to welcome poetry,
the fashionable toilet of the soul

Under the Carpet

O' sweet Jesus mortal strokes
but Bob O'Gavin can't find his wife

The undertaker tells him she is dead
He crawls under his carpet
He makes love to the linoleum
He whispers, "O'sweet Maria O'Gavin,
even your dust bunnies are brighter
than oblivion"

Praha, August 17th

It is the name of a dead girlfriend
The name of a suicidal kin
It haunts you like a dry beer
In the afternoon of a cool rain
It is the name of chills, of spines
Running in circles through your back,
Of your stomach imploding,
Of your youth laughing, tempting,
Taunting – your crotch thrusting
Toward it, thoughtlessly

It took twelve days to rain
In the streets people sang

You clutched the crotch of your pants
And asked if she, the dead,
The suicidal, the abandoned, the youth,
Would find behind the alcohol
A sober friend,
Pink pajamas,
A cruel and unusual seduction

Lullaby to the Looking Glass

There is a Tweedledee,
and Tweedledum,
and they ride the horseplay of proper nouns,
whistling all the while into oblivion
singing the praise of neon green beers.

They shake hands and tip
their hats to the hatter. They
smile that Carroll-chesh-don't-worry-
be-shire-happy smile, and poke
the bottoms of drunken umbrellas
up poor Alice's post-pubescent dress.

Later that day the Jabberwock won't play.
Air slithers through the nose of trombones,
quiet like a sneak, like a rapture,
like a single snowflake abrupt
on hot pavement.

Tweedledee and his brother dumb-
founded and tired retire to the living room.
They talk about Alice, about up her skirt,
about the pinheads twirling to the panic of orgasms.
The words yawn, and each comma like
an eyelid drooping tries to stop itself from sleep,
which like poems and souls never end.
Because poems are found in pinwheels,
and souls beneath the sofa cushions.

On the Bright Side

The churchyard was empty for birds.
The people were in the chapel
patched like pumpkins in mourning
for the squash,
flattened
two year-old Tim in the casket case.

He had without care,
and in the center of the street
stepped into that moving Subaru;

neither the driver the mother
the neighbor nor the officer
held his soul
and when the eyes went bare,
the body stiff and silent
the bishop claimed
god only knows what.

But the dead rustic chapel, inorganic and spiritless
chilled the late remains of Tim Holloway –
even Jesus on his stick, sinking into powder
painted no picture of remedial bliss.
Brother and sister were silent.
Still in their youth, they had not yet compromised
tragedy and testimony, remarking only dryly,
"Remember Tim, Jesus loves you."

The churchyard still empty for birds
and the things birds eat.

The Cremation of Old Patrick, Man of Many Beards

What a mess, most folks said
God the way they had spattered flakes
Of bone crust all over town

Praha, August 8th

The storm-sealed anxiety,
The green blood of grass
The happy villain in my throat

Neuchatel, Juillet 13th

What is that thing hating you there
where you keep that thing loving you?

Oh, it's the luggage of the life you left behind.
Wait. No. It's the sound of worms crying
just after a rainstorm.

Camus and the Call Girls

In the meadows of coffee beans
and the taxations of nicotine,
I am tempted to bring you over,

bring you back,
to the couch where we first kissed,
to that sweaty spot where sexy hopes
strangled our hearts into submission.

Instead, I drank
and sat in the cool edges of midnight
waiting for a call girl and licking
a stale pen for ink, hoping
before she arrived I might compile
something soft, something lonely,
like a worn toy you abandoned to
a box in the attic thirteen years ago.

What Gods loathe and angels love –
men pay not simply for sinful
adventures in midnight hours
but for a few hundred dollars confound
their hearts into believing that beauty,
sissy twenty-something beauty,
is theirs, and all that is made peaceful
by the trivial pride of prostituted attention.

Love is elusive, delusional, and
the heart weak with post-midnight madness
can compromise integrity for touch,
a testament to the apes in the trees who
flounder through life without this pretense
of purchases and diamond rings;
understand under the purple of stars
that men crave perversions, yes, penetrations,
but soft eyes, warm hands on shoulders
however pretended promise them more –
that they are not merely
the pear-shaped miscreants of mirrors;
that beauty is theirs, even everywhere,
even in the empty bowels
of dry and desperate evenings,

that we may find in the midst of empty summer nights
there is within us a

        sexy
        invincible
        thunderstorm.

Scientific Contribution

This proton meets this neutron
and sparks fly.
It seems the molecules are smiling
and kissing on porches.
I swear
they're holding hands in the hayfields,
necking upon necks.
The atoms are love-making molecules.
I swear
there is this tiny little world of love
only gods and microscopes can see.

Brain Sludge

There is weakness in these bones.
There is sadness in this brain.

There is serotonin and Tylenol,
wrinkled memories and alcohol,
names, dates, things
people places nicotine, paranoia
Speed,
in these thoughts; fear in the cortex,
the hippocampus, the hippopotamus
like the fat lard he is lazy
wading in the brain sludge
that is misfiring noumena,
that is silliness
death and terminal illness.

Your dead brother.
There is laughter in his bones.
There are worms in his brain.
There is his call from the dirt,
hungry inside the hippopotamus
for company.

There is death, and it is black.
It is the sludge the campus rolls in.
It is the absence between heart beats.
It is the jungle; it is the hunger.

Neuchatel, Juillet 12th

Revoila, the idealistic life of luggage –
lacking the ambitions of a nuclear economy
I find myself.

America, you understand, is traffic,
the traffic of fat people grinding their bones
against the weightlessness of the world

and I am only one hunded and forty pounds
when Franciska found me, when I found myself
back against the grain of America
She like a steaming glass of ice water, she
is breathing into my face and I have
found myself

Switzerland, vous apprehendez, is green,
the green of love, of vines and grapes and wine,
of humid lustful evenings and beer

but I am only one hundred and forty pounds
and still counting every goddamn blade of grass

Hungover

like a concrete anvil
metaphysics weren't upon me

I vomited
three days later
the pink latex still dripping from my lips
I pulled from my throat that sad cliche
about hindsight

and I reached above me
and flailing, found nothing
but a crispy bout of regret

I chewed carefully
so as not to upset my stomach

Strangers

Monsieur Meursault, I'll take your hand
despite its icy sickle flavor, and walk where you go.
I will steal your cell.
I will stand in your numb shoes and brace myself
naked against your faceless wall.
Cold stone may chill me, less it ravish me,
the nakedness of man and the greatly absurd.
We can embrace our fingers and scratch our eyes
and point our fingers at heaven,
pretending to damn Him. Damn Him.
We can laugh, Meursault. I'll laugh with you.
I'll love what is hard to love.
I'll reach inside you like a ghost and pull
where no one else will pull beneath your funny bones
a bottomless heart. There it is.
And if it isn't, I won't mind. I'll give you mine.
At night, we can remember Marie.
I'll touch you while you think of her.
To see you smile, a mammal smile, my God,
a smile! Where it is simple, so hard
for penalty-pushing people to see. My God, a smile!
The twitch of a joy, the spasm of life, the proof
of a grin, of a breath, of little mankind's emotion.
I'll steal her, if I have to.
And bring her late at night into your cell.
You can make love, and love, and live without that
melodramatic romance.
I understand you, Monsieur Meursault.
And if I didn't I would still. It's a decency thing.
When the morning comes when we walk from our life,
we make them so angry,
sure worshippers, presumptuous people, where life is
a mystery so easily solved we will lay our heads.
They quote Bible quotes.
As the blade like the hand of a pulpit pounder chops
through your neck, smile, Monsieur Meursault, smile
one last smile, give them nothing to achieve.
They will believe you a villain.
But do not satisfy them, do not platter them success,
give no solution to the howling mob of housemaking hatemongers.
Smile, Monsieur, smile, smile for the crowd, smile
on your beheaded head, it will twitter and collapse,
the muscle joy, the spasm, the proof, they'll take
in the name of their Father, of their callous Holy Ghost –
they'll steal your head because they're sick and human,
because the bloodshed is justified, they've got a great excuse.

Their strong testimonies, their heritage-assurities, their positive
identities may string us under nooses but we can smile, Monsieur,
and say twisted things about God.
One last good laugh before the snap, crackle, pop
of our necks.
Nothing is holy. Nothing is sacred. Man is man. This is proof.
Long after you've died, your feud's long-winded, they pray
you won't spread like a rock'n'roll lyric, you,
your different indifference have no place in a sophisticated,
meaningful, pompous, presumptuous God-believing,
judgment-wielding, justice-relishing mob of sweat-swallowing
businessmen who line the streets and pray every night,
who attend church every day but Super Bowl Sunday, refuse to root
for you, underdog, for you, tragedy, for Monsieur Meursault

because he is hard to understand, because he smiled but never cried,
because like a bad seed he threatened the good morality
of the good God-children; born unto this earth undoubtedly, indisputably,
who have since remained the most holy of mankinds ever
to kill one another for killing, to run home like proud soldiers
and politely knock-up their wives then kneel at their pretend bedside and
pretend – oh, how they pretend to judge each other flawlessly.

Monsieur Meursault, forgive us, for we know not where we send you.

Neuchatel, Aout 1st

you know what
when the sparklers are lit
when the fireworks rain
when that young couple beside you
is kissing and you're alone
you know what
when you find yourself
in a place where you can't find
anything about yourself
and you look to others,
yes, even to that girl,
and found is a foreign word
like paparazzi ou fille
and nothing means anything
you know that
you know when
and what, your life is
small and you see your reflection
in the blackness of the starlit sky
you know you are less beautiful
than a firework, than a cloud
than being found

Praha, August 27th

The watchband closes
and smothers your wrist.
You smell the smell of
sweat beneath it, of sweat
between your toes, of
sweat beneath your nails.

You are the foil, the opened,
the tin and plastic nonesense.
You are the residue.
You are the disease.

You swallow even hope
like a fat dogged horsepill.

The Brother of Prozac

At a time came upon him. He was on the move.

Made all these big decisions.
Made a lot of mistakes.
Made himself a fever. Made himself a headache.

Made himself a lot of memories.

It was she and he in the hot tub,
her legs pulling his shorts off;
her hand that knows him well.
It was her those months ago
with a wet rag patting down his hot body,
keeping him cool, keeping him.

And it was a gastrologist that gave him,
his little pill friends. Brothers.
Said with so many words, his illness, son,
was all in his head.

It's the fever. It's her fever.
It's a guilt like wasted time, like sad time
that an immune system and kidneys can't care for.
The cure, he knows and sees.
A hospital bed a few years down the road.
Tubes like her fingers pressed into his skin.
Doctors like love tearing him open, making him think,
making him dream about immortality.

Her picture on the stove and burning, his fever.
And the days after press down upon him,
he holds toward a fiery sky a new kind of rod.
A bottle of brothers, one day digested
struck down like love, like a tree, like a person.

And God's throne.

Praha, August 17th

an exclamation point changes
everything
even the meaning of
a sentence mid-meaningless
of a poem mid-coitus
of a girl sitting beside you
who smells like butter
cooked in a soft bourbon oil
like a girl you knew
long ago!
in a time before eternity

Crayon

The little purple crayon dog and his family
and their green scraped cloud of a tree.
The sun is smiling, and
smiling
like that damned don't worry be happy man.
Father, what a figure, and mother too,
sis and Ted and Baby Billy and the purple dog
like skeleton sticks, white
smiling faces,
branching columns that guard the two-story
American Dreamhouse.
The flowers are smiling,
as tall as the door,   I imagine Ted
cross-legged by the heat vent, crayons like scalpels
digging until the wounds stretch rainbows;
green blood scribbles the grass.
The purple dog like a sore thumb barks.
Ted smiles,
dreams of being married,
his home his office his cardiac arrest
                              dissected
in this, his
terribly paper world.

Neuchatel, Juillet 23rd

This cramped analytic brain
my memories beat against with the
fury of fifteen thousand gods.

The moon was full, blossomed, lonely
as it rose above the lac de Neuchatel,
basking its impotent rays upon us,
the migrants, the gypsies, the vagrants,
the vagabonds, the quacks.

I mean, really, yes, listen you, I don't know
but have you ever stopped to ask the dirt?

The Water of Autumn

the water of autumn
the seeds in a mess
the boys are indifferent
the women aren't dressed
most have been injured,
most even fall
soak in the water, boys
drown in your mess

Crowd

There's safety in numbers. Honeybee, how I admire
your bumping against the window pane, your refusal
to sting me on my arm.

Praha, August 25th

The taint of luke warm tea
dried on a small cedar table
reminds you an ulcer
near the back of your throat.
You try to spew but
acid dribbles from your mouth
and you smile like a jack-o-lantern,
carving a place for your eyes
in your corny neurotic skull.

Men Pigs

because his hands had tickled she shackled them.
he watched however curiously the blood
spin down his arm from his wrist over his chest
and it dripped from his pelvis to the his feet, like rain
down the branches of a bonsai tree, how he hung like a
bonsai tree. contorted distorted, she butchered him
with her kitchen knife. he dropped the money. it danced
on the floor. she grabbed his onions and tore them apart.
then urged him at gunpoint to see something really not there
that really was there. when he couldn't, she wrote him a poem
and walked an ugly purple carpet in his eye. the onions
she shoved down his throat, he nearly choked, at last
bruised enough to admit something where nothing was there.
he'd hold her hand and march miles with her
grinning nothing but agreeing all the way about the flowers
and the houses and the rings and the kitchens and the mirrors,
"yes dear" the mirrors, where, when she wasn't home, he would
stare with his hands on the dresser, braced, and into the mirror
face to face with himself for hours never seeing a thing

Neuchatel, Juillet 23rd

sur la lac, dan le lac
no one is here
nothing's concerned
it's a full moon over switzerland
but the floating corpse,
the bubbling babbling life,
the seething teeth
did you know tout le monde
everything burns
and nothing is loved

Praha, August 20th

Time is,
And it is
Playing games
Peak-a-boo in the bed sheets

Even here
He leaves behind a residue,
Shaven hairs in the sink,
A stench in the sheets,
The sad shadow of a
Poorly staged courage.

He cannot cry.
His tears are stuck somewhere
Behind his eyes.

Timing of Minors

what a wildly intellectual engagement it was
function form function form feet meter pieces
of ink painted on the page; oh Carlos Williams

as if the barrow were it able to tear out of the page
in blazing redness make morons of our muse,
blind everything but the greed of our humility

Wall

I've been taking these short strolls
late at night.

Pumpkin-patch houses lined up like soldiers,
stray off into the horizon and disappear.
Time will tell of a streetlamp,
of more houses,
of more abandoned sandbox toys,
bikes sleeping in the lawn,
and broken sprinklers squealing everywhere.

But what if it were a wall
and just ended.
A flat slab of nothingness.
An infinite oil-black aquarium, and I came upon it,
late at night, on one of my
midnight strolls.

And flicking it with my finger,
watch black tides ripple away in perfect circles.
And slapping my arm in it, like that crazy briar-patch rabbit,
tar-baby monolith, black waves cascade away
in all directions, and forever.
But my arm is gone.
And wondering how I might explain this –
I mean, no one will, I mean, believe, but just
gone and laughing at my stub,
slosh my other arm in for it.
I grope even for a finger that is nowhere.

My other arm is gone now, too.
Stepping back I see
a short reflection, of me without arms,
me with my potato stub lumps.
I laugh and, God, it is immense!
God. From a few feet back, God,
it is the end I'm staring into.
And real faint is the sudden sad cries
of a million tragic deaths, discarded dead people
bubbling and chewing on the flesh of my arms.

Among them, a childhood friend.
They said it was suicide, but casualty of what?
God and His big dumb battlefield?
It is death I'm staring into.
And having already taken my arms
I should jump through and in a devilish fury
bring everyone back to people who love them.

I stare into it a few minutes longer
before waddling away.
I'm frightened and tired and
like any other coward wish to return, while I can,
to those who love me.

These Priorities

I heard yesterday while I was wandering
down the road a small boy with chapped lips
scratching his friend Bill's head, "Valentines?,"
he said, "Shmalentines! Who needs stupid love?"
It made me laugh, so I sat on the park bench
next to a beautiful, beautiful woman.
I asked her if she'd like to get sushi.
She stared at me with very coated eyes
as a grin morphed into a smirk about her lipsticky lips.
Very briskly in fact she turned me down, very quickly
stood up and wagging her skirt like a tail between her legs
looked over her golden shoulder, and laughed.

I walked back down to the side of the road.
The boy with chapped lips didn't even ask me for money
but I gave him some and sat with his sort of homeless family.
"Who indeed," I said;
his friend Bill asked me to scratch his head
and I was more than grateful,
                              I was merciless.

Beware the Gulls

Years back and feeding only the sea life, admission
paid for as it was, and small fish at five bucks a pop –
naturally swift and hungry, infuriated the fathers,
those rotten gulls, scavenger, vulture, city-living grubbers
right in front of your face stealing the food and on the window
the guarantee, "Fish not Refundable
(and finer print) "Beware the Gulls."

Fours years later it must have been
and standing in the heat of July a boy named Stanley
prodding with a branch a broken sparrow.
Must have been the confusing wind speed, even traffic, pushed it to
bounce with the dull effect of a potato against the windshield
off, say, a school bus – and fallen from flight, it twitched
in the unshaded arena of a ten year-old boy,
whose boredom and heat have struck him so brainlessly
that some good torture might entertain the innocence of his heart.

I stand likewise just watching, more afraid than anything
to condemn the boy's cruel curiosity.
Afterall, his father runs the firework's stand ten feet away.
Afterall, it is just a bird
that rolls around on the ground now with a broken wing,
a clumsy take-flight, small and tidy bloodstains in the dirt.
It calms when it finds shade.

The sparrow now sheltered beneath my car –
"It is just a bird, Chris, and for Christ's sake! Just a bird" –
in reverse, pulling out, with a little hope
I might hear the pop of its body under the tire;
a small trigger and a small Lenny. I'm no man.
Even afraid of hearing death-crunch,
I run errands with this girlfriend and know even still
that Stanley might take it too far,
with thread to a bottle rocket, a firecracker up the ass.
July 4th is not far away.
We celebrate explosions.

Enraged fathers at five bucks a pop,
sons fascinated in their footsteps,
I couldn't help but think that my favorite boy had been
(and always would be) the one who turned from the dolphins,
to feed the sea gulls.

Dead Love and the Viola

And if I disappointed you
I would swish through the painted bricks,
the patio,
we built there together.
The expensive moonlight drops me his shovel
with a note on the handle,
it tells how sad he is
without his viola.
The shovel digs, and buries the bricks.
I politely bow, and wink at the moon.
Somewhere, below, deep beneath
the earth
maybe gatsby-corpses are dancing on our patio;
I'll pop my head in like an ostrich
and witness upside-down the final movement of a concert
dead love.
no one hands me the moon's viola.
I return it gratefully, and the moon winks as if to say
it must be someone else's turn.

Praha, August 7th

The earache is waiting,
The air is waiting
The molten yellow pastures of books,
They are waiting.
School is waiting. People are too.

Terror is the trumpet of impatience.
Like a knot in oak, like a twirl
In a tree stump, like the slow buzz
Of a fan rotating towards you.
The air is waiting.
Prague is waiting. The thumbnails
Of hope are waiting. And you,

You are lying in bed.
You are watching the moon.
You are afraid it can see you,
And you are afraid it cannot.
Loneliness is waiting.

God is laughing,
You should be too.

Sleeping with Nostalgia

she was a beautiful thing
of the past,
but then

all memories hang happily

the future unfolds his fingers
recklessly, one by one

Neuchatel, Aout 2nd

amongst the isle of breasts
swimming amidst the fluids
a lone boy is curious
and he asks a woman sun-bathing
why he has grown so hard and
yearning

she pushes him into the water
with an umbrella from the E.P.A.
laughing

and it seems proper,
sad, to be alone, frenzied;
to be a vacant little heart

Intercalaried Sex-Ed

In the crisp factorial of adultery,
She raised without thinking a hand, and asking

the stadium of virgins learning carefully
about the property between her legs

the slippiest secrets of men. Periods
and how to open so slyly, to still preserve

on schedule were changing, but the girl never leaving
those heralded men-magnets, halter-tops and faux-innocence.

and what with so many questions infuriating elders,
Still, at the crisp consideration of poets,

the principal was forced to dip her sadly
a person is escorted daily under that infertile thock

into a near breastless body. Her last words: "Why?"
of tombstones and faceless names, an epitaph that reads:

No one sleeps with a slut.
The Fundamentally Untalented. God Love Them.

Tomorrows

Much later than midnight, I sit naked.
A notepad and pen scribbles words
about empty beds and tomorrows.

In the bathroom, much later than midnight,
in the mirror a crack in my head appears.
I've tried to stuff my soul inside, but
it keeps blooming through.
It is beautiful, this fornication of feelings,
private, worse than the most sensual whispers.

Sprawled naked on your bed, idly
rubbing the crotch of your poem, capturing
nothing, not even the rapture and despair.

Praha, August 14th

The noise of complacency
Is the tickling of dead bodies
Or the smell of fat women

Today I walked through the maze
Chasing bagels and phone calls
Thinking for the third time

Familiarity is a Scottish accent
In a sitcom, in Scotland, in the Swiss
Foreign clouds of the Republic

They say, find yourself
And get lost
And find in your lonely weekends
Something larger than yourself,
Something larger than a pimple,
Something larger than a planet

They say, find yourself
In front of classrooms
Singing Scottish accents
Playmaking Canadian
Playmaking un-American

In the rain that relieved the heat,
In the sober mornings that followed
Did you find inside yourself
The aluminum courage to prod on

The noise of complacency
Is replaced by the gritting of teeth,
The loving hernia of resolved pain

El Rojo, el Blanco, y el Azul

Somewhere beyond the red
cracked sand,
beyond the arid prints,
a dogged cowboy boot, the knuckle-like
imprint of a stubborn spur –
beyond the whistling epics
of Ennio Morricone, I sat fawning
for their attention.

Beneath the shrill white
ivory palms
the girls bathed in black oil,
gently caressing the corners
of impossible-to-reach places,
giggling about breast sizes,
maple-color-coated rock titties,
horse power and pom poms.

Above the sacred blue
Bromine-controlled pool
I sat fawning, with the men.
We drank petroleum,
swallowed Cialis,
and launched our penises skyward,

Somewhere,
a radar blips and assures us
no children nor schools nor
churches nor cemeteries,
no galleries nor museums nor
upright businesses nor innocent
patrons –

and we mingle yet in our orgy,
firing away our wads from satin sheets,
watching our women doused
in a higher-quality-of-life,

drowned,
of somewhere beyond.

Jihlava, September 16th

Thirty-six days and
one juicy lie later
you sit in the grease
and revel the stench
of dirty laundry
in Jihlava.

A man named Ales
showed you kindness.
A woman named Misa
showed you beauty.
And yet you stuck it to them
screeching, laughing
with your middle finger like a tail
between your legs.

Thirty-six bites later
the bed bugs do the mambo
in your pubic hair.
They sing you songs
about Jihlava,
about dirty laundry
and luke-warm gratitude.

Of Cancer

Father was never clean-shaven
when the wrinkles began
and the bone started tugging his skin inward
tightening the sheet around his face.

And when his hands shriveled
they twitched silently like dying pets –
ferrets, perhaps
father was unwilling to commit to sleep.

Praha, August 7th

In the terminal I heard the pundits,
the terrorism and alerts, the fear
from the true-blue fellow beside me.

It is dripping pus. It is gravitational.
New York and Prague smell the same.

My luggage was lost,
my hope dangling from my sleeve.
I could only sneeze, cry,
waste, and claw at Pilsner Urquells.

The note from my mother, it tried.
But my brain was already bathing
in the earnest cheap thrill of crawling
back naked into the womb,
onto my cross.

Published

The night you slept on the floor
you never heard the world turning around you.
Don Juan crawled inside her womb,
and spun her uterus like a Wheel of Fortune.

He's crawled now inside so many,
gambling,
and never happier anyhow than you,
yet
you oggle his good looks and charm
with a jealousy that can slice bread
or hearts.

He's mistaken himself for Quixote.
And you grow exhausted
of watching les filles and female forms
you longed to touch turn towards him.

It is no different than anywhere.
You stare at Pauline, who stares at
Jimmy or John, who stares at Ginny,
who stares at the beer-bellied host
of poetry, of Quixote, or Juan
stupidily flinging himself towards mills
that grant passage only to the lonely.

There is regret in a room.
There is heartbreak between strangers.
It is a sissy moral universe
that binds you to hope, love, and
creeping sadistic optimism.

We dismiss feelings.
We do.
From the inclination, the
haunting accidental car accident,
to the notion that she's the one;
feelings are scrap paper,
the heart is a crumpled and failed
piece of art.

Lana remembered your name
never three times.

And you should allow
a 3.625" x 1.25" space in the bottom
right hand corner of the back cover.
This will be where the barcode
of your now sellable displeasure
will be placed.

Father

It is a sour, nostalgic November day
and somehow these sixty-year old synapses,
befuddled by age and rain and newspaper pages,
are reminded of the times you believed in Jesus.

On my shoulders I would carry you.
You wore simplicity, sweaters
of Saturday morning cartoon characters,
and spoke of nothing that couldn't be solved
by the thin inquisition of childhood want
and imagination.

As we moved along, your grasp on my graying temples
would slip and you'd hold your hands high,
reaching for ozones or sunsets or promised blue skies;
Your laughter absolving the lies, the crimes,
the cruel and unusual disquiet of science,
you'd spread your arms wide,
like you too had been crucified
to the spirit and slight of blind assurance.

During the grace of that fragile moment,
because nothing is small and nothing is harmless,
with your mouth open wide you swallowed a fly
and your mother and I with nursery rhymes in mind
took you in our arms laughing, but

on this cold November day, knowing you now,
and knowing you then, my apologies son –
I never expected you to be so sad, so serious
but that hint of suspect in your childhood eye
after that silly bug stole your smile,
pleaded with me to promise that things would
and could be perfect again,
that the order your mother and I manufactured
wouldn't haunt you like the God we gave you,
that the loss of innocence wouldn't be so happenstance,
so ridiculous, so trite and tragic
your young and callow existential crisis.

Hope is a dirty, bewitching little tune
we hum in our heads as we gamble.
Because unlike God we must as parents
dare to throw dice in this wanton and willless universe.

Revelation 22:19

fat little bible in the light
of what culture is your leather?

you look like a raisin, you and your
coiled flesh wrinkles bruises
of what have you made man
in the madness of an everlife
the red gold linings of your pages
and that frightened golden Holy
tattooed in your surface like
fresh footprints in dirt like
sad scars above crocodile eyes

you brick of hope you
weightless morality
what hands have oiled sweated
pressed you close to the face
kissed that manlike binding cursed
treasured you and of more worth
than the human heart, of what history
do you regret?

remember when I in my godless gratitude
arranged you under fiction,
we laughed and every bent word
told of bullshit; we had nearly forgotten
what a word was, what a word would be
nothing but skepticism is your skin
yet between inches is god and hell
and every dimple in between

angels with stolen halos

Jihlava, September 12th

The holy trinity returns tomorrow.
The sky is red.
And the world is watching the skies
with apocalyptic anticipation.

On your mobile your mother phones
to tell you she loves you.
You cannot hear her.
The wild laughter of the world condemned
drowns out even your memories –
you curled in your bed, fetal-like, soft,
thrusting gracefully in a hot tub with that girl,
driving naked down seventh avenue –

you'd think folks would be crying,
would be on their knees praying.
But their laughter is mysterious,
contagious, audacious, flirtatious.
"C'mon, God! Show us what you can do!"

You will not be around for last call.
You will not welcome Jesus into your arms.
You will be in a tea shop somewhere, possibly
in the beauty of Czech Republics,
on the mobile with your mother
clawing desperately at the memories
she fed you for centuries with her breast.

Deeply Religious

Eons after midnight, as the moon laughed,
and the rabbits waltzed in the fields,
he snuck into barns,
and chewing on the corners of chipped paint,
he knelt and prayed atop coarse golden hay.

He was approached by angels with stolen halos;
they would berate him for tossing like potato chips
the dried red paint into his mouth.

But they rather enjoyed his prayers,
and thus granted him the blessing of superstition,
which consists of two eggs over-easy,
a lightly browned messiah, three sides of faith,
coated in a heavenly glaze of pathos
and peace.

Jihlava, September 16th

It is strange, she thinks
sitting in the street
hearing the blithering-blathering
speech of someone she cannot
tell from Adam. She crosses her legs.
And smiles curiously
when it begins to rain, as though
she'd had some influence
on the darkening sky, as though
crossing her legs was a sly motion,
a lazy rain dance to the gods, as though
tossing her hair over her shoulder
condensed everything wet and dry,
as though the thunder was her laughter.

Sin

Drove like a bat outta helluva maniac
passed by three women all keeping themselves
spread open on a curb bench.

Pulled that motorcycle to a stop, lifted sunglasses
from his face to lap, winked, put them
on again. Said, "Sorry girls, you angels

too damn bright for me to see. Gotta
shade my eyes. Gotta ask you if you're happy."
For a price you might be too, they answered.

My friend, this motorcycle man smiled.
"Girls, I found everything I need to live right now.
I say it's enough to know you'll always be here."

And he almost got a blowjob, but believing he saw
a small melancholy in her eye stopped her mouth,
placed his hands upon her head and

asked God if he'd bless her. Asked God, make her happy.
Noticed then that it looked like rain, that he suddenly
ached to orgasm, and with his hand was relieving himself.

The girl just watching said, "Sir, you ain't no saint."
Zipping up, he said, "No, ma'am. Hope never to be.
I'm so close to God He can't even see me."

Jihlava, September 22nd

There was something I was going to say
but I lost it in the ether
of passing by a small pub
where beer costs only crowns
and the gardens are soft with rain.

It had something to do with irony,
but irony now is distant
like the dark blue storm on the horizon
softy crackling with thunder,
softly laughing with godly pride.

In the Beginning there was the Feud and the Table

The round table rolled and walloped God in the head.
The knights and people running it like a tire
had not seen Him sitting among the thorns
munching daisies.

God and His head bumped solid like a squash the dirt
where his fat feet pricked in and about roses
and puncturing His little piggy at the market
went all His hot air.

Like a flat pancake, they sat the table upon Him and
King Arthur commented, "Tis a fine rug shaped
like a moral we have built this kingdom upon."
God's poor muffled voice trembled bitterly the surface
and jiggled the castle the boys fashioned delicately
with poker cards.
                                        His voice shook
but they all were just gentle, like feathers,
polite Englishmen talking about the weather, the world,
and justice – the castle, finished, a lofty Babylon, and God
like the flat pancake He was huffed and puffed and blew
apart the castle of futile playing cards.

The knights and all having realized what they'd done
removed the table and borrowing Thanatos' bicycle-pump
stuffed up God some more. His voice shook. King Arthur
courteously offered Him a seat at the table but
God refused and stamped them all to hell.

                        Then,
while neither Adam nor Eve was looking lifted the table
and took it for His own, stopping only to graze the daisies
on his way.

Ravenclark and Dante

The Bible he speared with a pitchfork, Ravenclark,
at the moment when God had been sipping His wine.

It was Judgment Day (also Ravenclark's birthday)
and when asked about the crime, he sighed –
"I feel that the hunt was hilarious, Lord. But
the scarecrow made me do it!"

And the scarecrow, being as if he only had a brain,
and with little defense for himself, brought only the clacks
(the ravens stuck to his back, and his arms).

It was Judicial,
but God afterall being a Wise Guy
sent with the ravens clacking and Ravenclark clapping
poor scarecrow to Dante, who,
as an official failure on the study of forgiveness
cashed in a few good notions on the topic of being mean,
devised a most efficient form of contrition for this man made of straw
and in need of a brain.

He placed poor scarecrow now stuffed with staples
along the Holy Road, the Free Spirit Express-way.

And God at a moment of youthful anxiety had taken for a ride His trike.
All according to Dante's plan, the scarecrow stuck to the rim,
and God at last stranded in the middle of nowhere,
there, at last, there, where Dante planned to take upon himself
even the sins of another world.

My Woman of Faith

It's time for you to take me, my
rattlesnake sheddings, between your lips.

Will you whisper spirits up my nose?
Will you take and rub my hand in the grass?
Will you palm it, read it, tell it sordid silly
smart theistic things?
Thorned crowns and allergies.
Tickles? Or genes or faith or love or will,
yes, will you wean me, face and flesh
against your celestial breast?

They say you carry for me even
the weight of the cross, the burden of
tendencies. Indeed, even, they do say
allergies and hairs and spirits
in that nose.   Olfactory saviors
and hallucinators.

They say you see like a sixty-watt
bulb beneath a baby's ear
beyond the nostril a neon glow of soul;
they say, through the cornea, a kind of
                    oblivion.

              Last weekend,
we almost drowned. We floated on the ocean.
The sun was hot. Our skin now peeling.

I wonder, you, maybe, my woman of faith –
if I laid my head in your lap,
could you peel the dead skin from my forehead?
Would you hold it close to your lips and
blowing it into the wind prove,
that it, that I, that my skin falls somewhere
for a reason, for a rhyme?

The Zelihoof and Genesis 7

The Zelihoof
was not exactly Cain nor able
to speak out as animals can't against supreme beings.
Instead it died and disappeared and being that
it all just might be a myth, never one of his fossils
round happy teeth or glad empty eye sockets
were uncovered. Then full and bright white with instinct
the Zelihoof's eyes were fixed on the heavens
like the why-sad twitch of a horsetail
stung with saltwater and smeared with innocence
when the Zelihoof's zebra-mouth stretched open
and his hollow wordless bellow, shriek like a magpie
choking on the wake, well, that fat ark just kept trailing away.

Some sinners then when the whole thing began
had some time to wrap their arms around the Zelihoof.
Its legs were strong against the current and paddling
like a dozen men as it were, sinners took refuge around his neck
on his back at his tail at his gray face and prayed,
well, not to God, I would guess
(He had disposed of them)
but to chance or to luck or to the devil himself.

Mean families hugged each other beaten children swarmed
at their terrible parents legs newborn demons in diapers
sucked at their mother's sopping breasts weak prostitute women
and lying stealing beating dying men shrieked for mercy.
Save Noah and Friends, and a Few Good Mammals,
sterilization raining cats and dogs, liquidation taking care of the world,
sinners and Zelihoofs choking down their just desserts
under the great downpour of rain and pain and
eternal justice that atomic like sweet-soap-sopping night.

God gave His kids a rainbow:
promise sign apology, apocalyptic appraisal –
for the record just look how beautiful a holocaust can be!

And no wonder things keep stinging, what with the sand and trees
rivers and mountains fertilized by the ashes of those un-mourned.
It is a countless thousand bodies strung all over the sky
and sprinkled with the species, last of her kind, Zelihoof dust
still settling on our eyelids, our fingertips, our Bible covers.

Praha, August 13th

Rotting,
Dull gray and uninspiring
In the skylight Irene descends
She frames your future
In a fruitbasket
She lays Catholic hands upon you
And chews bottlecaps

The end of the week yawns
And swallows the universe entirely

Glowing Screen Ode to Loneliness

He stood corrected and dripping urine.
It was October 29th and new snow, sleazy memories.

What the furnace didn't seem to be working and all,
His chilled body frozen thin in the mirror
And that appendage aching forward like a dead rat
Choking out kidney syrup between clenched crow's feet.
That man, he was dying.

Left across the hall under black drapes a Macintosh
In plain sight and what why shouldn't it be when there that boy was
With his head in the window like a potted plant, his chin on the sill
His breath sticking to the window with each goddamned heartbeat.
He read that glowing screen Ode To Loneliness
Was what it was called and really only twelve
That boy didn't understand a thing except, boy, the Ode was sad
And came to so little a conclusion it made him lick the window.

It was only years later with fragments did the boy grow up.
Knew at least one thing for sure and that was nothing
That at least the poem had said and gone something like this
Though never published:

I stand corrected and dripping urine
It is October 29th and the new snow reminds me of her
In and out of the hut tub, her hand rubbing me
Her lips taste like butterscotch
And she always waited with a smile when I had to get
Her stain out of my pants.
I miss her now. Guess at least my kidneys must also.
They are beginning to swell more than my penis, I swear.
Better to be back a kid again where scraping knees
Hurt until it fell into nowhere near the heart
Never like these years now clog arteries and steal semen.

And signed and dated the boy knew the author though
He died what three months later not of kidney clogs but suicide.
Stared still like a plant from his window at the stretcher frightened
Not by the bloodstains or neighbors running, but by thinking
What happened to a person's things when they die?
That man the boy knew lived alone and his Macintosh wherever it went
Disappeared and with it the soft glowing Ode to Loneliness.

94

And struggle as he might have the rest of his life to think that man a fruitcake
Knew that poem, goddamnit, by heart and feared even still at nineteen
By some sick twist of God and fate and sinister paradox
The man in the stretcher and author in his own little world would be
His father never.
Said and thought that man's suicide should fall hard upon us
More so even than the fall of Adam, or likewise
It is absolutely nothing that cleans off hope of living and loving forever
And taken sooner than we'd like I guess he just dug himself sooner.

That man? Was he my father? Of course not and still yet maybe
Just like his poem was a worthless pile of artistic bunk
It is perhaps the loudest laughter in a worldless beauty.

Oscillating

God didn't like Galileo; what a mess in his banister tower
writing himself a biddy bible, like a lever stepping
onto a table and swinging his arms like pendulums –
pretend, God! oh, pretend-god, this is my sermon on the mount.
Laid down some concrete commandments,
about the sun, the moon, and some other stuff;
poking his head out a window, spitting up at the sky,
there was the gravity. Through wet vision the top, the tip
of his prison, tip-top of his tower of Babel.

Tired and back through the door to homes, God, they go and
you tell us we're not oscillating? But we are, God. God, we are.
Oh God, are we ever.

Against My Will

Praying is sex for the soul he said, old saintman never heard
nor met on the street with boards like bread sandwiching each side of him.
Was waving his hand around about God, that cracker,
that cheese in a cracker, between those boards of conviction, religion,
yet still he seemed a tolerant man.

About fifty and tiny and tired, a Bible like a baton bouncing in his hand
up and down with a saintly profound performance
he called upon God to give man peace, forgive the fallen,
swear to the Almighty the allegiance of the meek, the mild, the weary,
the wasted.

        "And I don't want a
goddamn pamphlet," a woman named Irene was irate.
This struck me as funny so I asked for a pamphlet.
He smiled and told me he didn't really believe in God,
that he had called his wife Sunflower, that she had enjoyed many men
and that the thought of her in hell would keep his eyes in scriptures
like sickles, sad, bent, and prayer was something he preached only
because the sky would never be blue.

I told him about the Tao.
He told me Eastern Philosophy turns brains into trees.
Love Jesus, friend, love gravity, give your brain a hand at creation,
he was saying, that if indeed God made man,
man alone made God worth keeping.

My Sin

God if love exists has been
my fault forever analyzing you,

was what he said
the temper with which he had slain
the big man, for things in books
had tested him and he was tired of
passing

then for some reason liked love
and the idea of idling beside Him

Working

let the living, the gooey afterlife go
stare each second in the mouth
place the cross in the closet

run around your naked streets
smiling and frenzied

For Isaac, even Abraham, Judas, also Jesus

All the whole while life went by.

I stuffed myself here. Cried, God,
I'll never love your nothing.

Still can, like yesterday, dad
with a hard hand on my shoulder
saddling his ass,
riding us up to a far off commandment.

I asked him, hard at work on the altar.
A tall and quiet man; eyes like,
eyes like sandpaper, chest like noise.
To make things simpler took the knife,
sharpened it against a sharper stone.
I asked him, father, I said, "Father,"
and thinking of the blood and the lamb,
knew when those sandpaper eyes
folded in on themselves and that chest silenced
by the great weight of the sky above.

He turned his back to me, said, "Son,
I know you will never run."

So I ran.

Left him there and saved the trouble,
the knife and my father sharpening, used like tools.
I found the devil as a serpent, hard as a log.
He was hungry and I knew now, could feed even the fools.
Crawling inside his big sinful belly
and with my abandonment, guilt, ruin and loving crest
cut a hole with the tip of my fingernail. Watched even
years and years go by. Felt bad for none of them,
except for one, and he was
so far away I don't even know his name.
But like a cradle he walked gentle, seemed to
put his arm around everyone he met.
And I did,
I felt sorry for that man.
Then the sky rumbled. Saw the pain on the thorn-crowned fetus;
knew that God had gone and done it all again.

I use my sins here. They keep me nice-like, hidden.
Thinking sometimes, still like a childhood stolen,
I could muster even enough lightning to strike God down;
fall from the sky, fall even onto His big dumb battlefield.

It's a sad thing all over the place. Keep hoping
for a better world plan than pain, keep thinking Peace in a captain-hat
might come along and give it all a rest.

Safe here at last, at least until I die.

Born Again

In God's name,
the paper sky is pretty

I ran after Him down the conveyer
but what appeared to be a crumb of His soul
was only
a little scripture

Lauterbrunnen, July 27th and Neuchatel, July 29th

Now, is it the women
or the world
moaning beneath your conscious
tickling your blue balls?
Is it the women or the world
you're aching to sleep with?

In a canyon, in the jungfrau,
in the young frost of the swiss,
amongst the sky cascading into the valley,
a trumpeting seed was planted.
The oceans sacrificed themselves
to grow a little slice of growth, to
bask in the wind of the waters.
And no one knew about bones or blood.
The tombstones reserved for retirement,
for a garden, for a kindergarten.
And beyond the peaks and the peace
in Oregon, say, or maybe Wales
a woman is beaten and raped.
A bomb in Israel slices some children into dust.
In third worlds, a dozen people vomit poverty
over one another. In America the millionares
make another million and
a plane explodes, an ozone implodes,
a building slaughtered, a city slit its throat.
And the blood from the death of everywhere-else
carves its way through the world,
(if Christ were proselytizing now
he'd tap his beer bottle against your own
wishing you health, happiness, and a sandbag).

But the sky pours into Lauterbrunnen
and the growth of growth is peaceful.

Beauty does exist

if only for a mile if only for a month
and you really must ask yourself:
is it the women or the world
you're yearning to fuck the life back into?

Inert God

above the sky
and folding it over her eyes,
the entire time.

He had no one he loved with blood,
spineless as a spirit,
holy-heartless as a ghost;

she made love to many men
and loved maybe one of them.
It was her legs that kept keeping
money between the purse and
despite the noise of a sexless frenzy
she hung above her bed
above his head
as he moved into her, a cross
and never could forget who
had stoned who had stoned no one.

At orgasm he was busy
but she was flimsy and gawk-eyed,
wondering why the world was
the way it was with pain.
The thorns in his head, and wept nails
along his wrist and hands;
his legs curled
in on themselves like a newborn, eyes
up at heaven and whimpering, God
have you forsaken him? Yet, even still,
wild and screwed she flung
the man atop her off her,
told him to stick it some place else.

Screamed and swallowing pills
pulled herself together towards the bed
and knelt with trembling hope,
told God she could never love Him,
took Jesus into her heart,
dropped the cross into her mouth.

She pleaded to know why suffering sins
must pain people at all in the end.
And with a hand to her breast
consumed Christ with life

as her last breath left those lips,
Malicious God, inert God, tragic God
took her into His arms and did with her
whatever whenever He willed.

Christ in her belly wailing.

a brutal and sexy oscillation

Salt Lake City, August 20th

I will be you in the sandbox,
you, your pirate ship
Your sweet pickled childhood
is mine as I wade through this
mush, this stuff growing on trees
There is a girl

This cascade of commercials,
this tide of tight-asses,
this new virgin world won't
stain the sheets, won't
spread its beautiful blue curtains
pour toi
There is a girl

She the world we mean copulates,
placing my heart in her bathwater;
that I did was had now done ain't no more
and so more than still and god I miss
sommeil avec la pluie
There is always a girl

Little to be had here whimpers
a beautiful blue newborn belief

The Purple

It was cold and late when she called.

He asked if she had noticed
the purple haze in the sky
two weeks prior;
it had settled over the city
and turned everyone to stone.

He told her about the girl
now granite and gasping
he had been making love to,

how he keeps her
in his living room,
how late at night sitting on the sofa
he strokes himself softly
to the sparkling emeralds
he laid over her eyes,
to the blood of a white rat
he used to paint her lips,
and the flesh from his thigh
he carved gently and laid
over her cheeks.

"Did you notice," he asked again,
"that two weeks ago,
when I met her,
and the purple passed over,
and everything froze?"

She hadn't noticed. And hung up
yawning; it had been a long day,
and work came earlier tomorrow
than it had for thousands of years,

when men trimmed their beards
with clam shells, and women
kept their feet warm
with lucid dreams of deer meat
and caviar.

La Même Chose

In the dim glow of celluloid death,
the back of their hands rested together.

She was beautiful and shy, like a
cinder in snowfall.

And doubts remain, as doubts do,
and so their hands reluctant to entwine
rested together, frightened,
numb with delight – two magnets
separated by a thin gloss of worry,
softly oscillating between poles, hope
and hesitation.

Jessica

It was a pristine morning at the gallows.
You and I, we'd been in love now for seventeen hours,
for less than a day, for an eon of novelty,
for a lifetime of daydreams, and doubt.

You wore a blue summer dress speckled with promises
and dug your heels into the simmering summer soil.

I wore a necktie. I'd wanted to look my best.
And holding hands beneath the snapped jiggling bodies,
shadows of death danced over our eyes; we smiled.
You whispered, "We are forever." And I thought about
the permanence of kissing your inner thigh.

Do you remember the last time we made love,
ripples of red wool beneath a blazing sun,
legs gliding between and above and over,
intwined, sweet, sweaty, pressed, desperate
for the day we had watched death holding hands?

We were two symbionts in a sleeping bag,
doused by heat, and young, and do you remember
the little boy in the Digimon sweater? He
pointed at our cocoon and asked his mother,
"How large can caterpillars grow?"

It was a pristine morning seventeen months later,
still, when our short-lived love skirted away –
your high heels now dug your hope into other men,
and I chased frantically in camoflague the fleeting
apathy of proposals and promises, of Cupid stupidly
firing away his wad like a drunken sniper.

But it was war,
I had found a wheelchair and you a wedding dress.

And yet now you arrive at the doorstep,
bringing like loaves of French bread
my legs sticking out of a brown paper sack.
You smile, and are saying sweet things about the past.

Somehow, this begins painting the resolve,
all the pain we had pigeonholed
for seventeen eons now slips through the paper-thin pours
of our skin.

The relentless frenzy of life can be frozen;
the lurid illusion of anger buried by even one butter-fingered
misstep near the brink of apology.

As if to say, it is so much to say, "You know what?

We felt love.
And I am sorry."

Neuchatel, Juillet 11th

Outside the window, a faucet drips
I am bathed in sunlight
forgetting the gray bones of America

Franziska cuts like a paper snowflake
a Swiss-shaped hole in my heart
and I am heavy, like a pine needle

Tense Messages

Hi Chris. This is Melanie.
I'm that girl who you think thinks
might be interested in screwing you;

and you've no way of knowing
whether my blank gaze was waiting
for a kiss, or thinking of
waterloos and dandelions
and then you were in my face and
unable to stop without half-assing your effort

we kissed for hours on end.

Then, when you're away
I return softly to my waterloos, my dandelions.

Jihlava, September 30th

It seems as a man
I write about man things.
Like butt cracks above trousers,
like visible panty lines, like the smell
of sour tobacco on her breath.
Like the want you have
for her to stick you in her mouth
and roll you around like a wet balloon,
a cartoon drunk happy and gawk-eyed
at everything.

Yes. I cannot help it, mother.
I notice her thighs and her eyes
and I think of all the possibilities,
the perverse universe in between.

September Something

I am a fetus inside myself.
The rain smells of pine, sweat, and soul,
and sticking to your neck reminds you
of hickies and peace.

You are thinking of a woman,
of her thighs around your neck,
of wet genitals against your lips, and
peace.

The rain-soaked cigarette sticks to your lips,
and you think to yourself that love is
a smokescreen; you remember rings,
thoughts of forever, of sickness and health,
of bullshit and blowjobs, of God scampering
across the clouds like a frightened field mouse.

Doubt makes its bid for a better world,
but you threw up blood, and pissed on puppies.

Promises have a half-life and
in the rain you are a fetus inside yourself.

Praha, August 29th

The breeze is small but sly
passing over you easily
like a lotion
or a tonic.
You're thinking about her,
about your one-to-one love,
about the small memories
she gave you in a tin box,
about the sour nostalgia
of daquiris in dixie cups.

Remember the motions?
The way she tossed her head back
like the seizures she had when young
tossed to and fro, to show
how ridiculous mechanical music,
computerized beats
like the sad synchronized march
of a military – she showed you,
remember,
what life would be like without melodies.

Praha cried all last night.
That kind, unreserved city let loose
a wail of laughter and tears
at your plight.
You are almost out of deodorant
And the waft of your dreams
is entertainment for the post-communist hope
of first-stressed syllabic names
like Barbora, like the girl on the street
handing out porn pamphlets who paused
to kiss you twice, once on each
and every thorn on the cynical side
of your face.

Remember the motions,
the weight of suitcases,
the small room that housed you
from the rain and the tears
and encased your smell like a subway
of athletes sweating something dark
like dirt,

like the marrow dripping straight
through their bones.

Remember your home?
It is like a polaroid now, fading
wilting,
developing backwards through time.

Nearing Dawn and Stacy

In the mornings I drink Stacy.
She tastes of beauty,
and is a body of whiskey.

My ceiling drips nostalgia. It's white
but blotched and spatted with
semen stains and hope.
My eyes are closed.
My mouth is open.
and I can feel the wet strands
trickle through my throat laughing.

In the evenings is the whiskey.
It recalls the taste of Stacy
and her untouchable body of beauty.

Praha, August 10th

There are beautiful girls.
There are sirens in the stupor.
There are drinks in the ozone,
Martinis from Mars,
Cool blue vodka like a light rain
Dangling from the twilight.

She leans in through the noise,
Whispers something about something
And the two of you balance
Armchairs and Boston on your ears,
Softly entwining your language
In the vacuum of your new vicinity
There is only the two of you and
The universe stumped
His toe laughing at your hope,
At your beard,
At your confused blue mucus.

The twilight with cool air as its ally

Narcoleptic Love

Him
leaning
in love.

Saw a medal in the mud puddle
in his bed, beside his head
as he awoke.
And with red eyes took a finger
slipped it through the loop
and lifted it like a sick sock
where he stared.

Her
thrusting
another body.

In another bed, her head
was screaming for that thing to
move her.
She was humping his poor pelvis
squeezing her eyes seeing her
fucking a beautiful man
far from below her.

He listened to her shower.
The blankets sprawled like rags across the bed.
The sweat still steaming, stinging
his hurt was spent and wet and lamented,
squeezing his eyes, seeing him
like a madman in a ballroom, swish her
swoosh her, dip her, envelop her,
and spin her.

His eyes real, red and open, reading
the engraving engraved on her necklace
he had like that madman ballroom man torn
from her neck under the play
that he was a beautiful man.

He was her thirty-second and new and thin.
Through the cum stain gravy pain mud dripping
off the corners of the heart, was everything.

Neuchatel, Juillet 10th

ensuite
the photographs in my pants
of your horror
my soap-stained underwear
young dreams are cherry-popped
squozen, sapped of nectar,
drained in the melting pot of America

neuchatel, dix juillet
ensuite
the photograph of my life
your horror
my whitewashed underwear dreams
drenched in an orgasmic flood of
premature ejaculation
yes
ensuite
my, the photograph in my pants,
in neuchatel, Franziska, still
staining my lunettes du soleil, still
stuffing my stuff with nectar

ensuite,
I'm back, eons from home
eons from young
squozen is not a word and I
well I
have a photograph in my pants
and am therefore resilient

Neuchatel, Juilliet 11th

jesus it smells gorgeous outside
but franziska,
franziska is one floor away
and dreaming a different dream
and i, well, i
am feeling less resilient

Lake of Lucid Meaning

Lonely women, men
in breezing fields of kisses
waves of brush just fucking each other;
walking by, whistling
the elms tip forward and foreshadow
the grass grows like an erection
and the godawful stream peddles along
aimlessly, relentlessly
where they follow it
and meet
and drink
from the lake of lucid meaning.

Lovers lone and alone,
the sun sweats his gooey sperm upon them
and they sprawl out to claim cancer
thankfully.

All Too Personal

Sitting with my shirt off, shedding
The smell of smoke like the peel of an orange.
I miss her – her, and her cheats, her
Monopolizing life, her two stupid dogs
Chasing and eating and shitting and making
Filthy an otherwise healthy relationship.

I miss her cheating on me; I miss
The way she lied and said she hadn't.

I miss sex; yes, sex, with her –
Quiet and important – and her brother
Slithering around the house, a
Well-intended snake, or saint, some
Profound twenty-times interpretable
Biblical allegory of our counterfeit
Relationship.

The things we had, the things we didn't;
The healthy way to bemoan a lost love?

And despite everything that could mean
Everything, I worry about her. Love her.
Miss her.
Forsake her, and forbid her.

Jihlava, September 30th

Without underwear in her
neon green passing
she asks you for pivos
and you graciously accept
even ten minutes from teaching.
How could you say no to that sly crack
smirking at you above her trousers,
how could you satiate the eternity
that is home yet between you
and this pivo and this girl
floating around in a neon green sweater?

Jung's Misanthrope

There is something everywhere that slides behind love
and he doesn't know what it means or where it goes.

Used to as a child learn at Sunday School about God.
It was at the same time in fifth grade *fuck* was being taught
and always taking the name in vain on weekdays
church was a quiet time, not for reflection but for jittery muscles
aching to slide and laugh and toss themselves,
children banging baseballs and spitting storms and
happy to say *fuck* when striking out. God
all the while just above and beyond and amused, maybe,
it was *fuck* through Friday and stifled life on Sunday.

Girls and God and sports and recess and
adventures at the front porch on mowed grass,
fence-climbing before bed time
and sometimes they remembered to kneel
and sometimes they didn't.
Remember, talk to that powerful man, invisible man
asking now as puberty prods along for Misty's eyes
Jessica's, Marie's, Candy's, Mandy's, Crystal's,
their prayers erecting and gripping hope for love,
all the boys fat and thin, good and bad, begin
that long haul hope for interest and upset stomach
conquest and score, kiss from the first cheek to the pussy.
God's been adopted for love and just like Himself
teenage boys grope for things unseen.

Masturbation the Bible tells at Sunday School especially
something the great man held little appreciation for.
The boys now tired of fence-hopping and adventures
ache just below their belly and find that stroking
wets the bed and dribbles guilt all over the place.
Sometimes they remember to pray before jacking off
and sometimes they're afraid to remember.

God must be a lot of things, the world curls in
and a lot of good people cup their hands over truth
while a lot of grown boys never snicker, admit, or whisper
to that mysterious wife beside them
about how sex slipped in so early and stole
the grass adventures and imaginations
and how, "God, pray she loves me though she doesn't know me,
God, pray she loves me despite the appetite that swallows her whole."

Pubescent boys praying at their bedside, because it's empty
the future more than God and like childhood slides behind
an imaginary indent on the mattress pressing her shape,
her curves, her beautiful sexuality. His future.

He renames her silhouette God and asks only that it be love
his thin arms embracing himself and everything unsure.

Neuchatel, Juillet 22nd

acetaminophen may cause liver damage and
friends may deliver you unto ridicule,
consciousness or Liverpool, maybe Lauterbrunnen
where you find the water falls from the sky,
yes, in torrents, from the agnostic god's eye
upon your homeless head and face,
upon your stale embrace
and, yes, acetaminophen may cause liver damage

yet there is no warning outside of acetaminophen:
girls too may cause swelling, reddening, and
irritation.

Late

1:00 a.m.

His antenna like spaghetti noodles
draped across his television
translated nothing but the raw
crackling of dead leaves piped
through waves of post-midnight
madness, the buzz of organs
humming across walkie-talkies
chattering about charred fish floating
from a sea of white prepositions –

Moving one noodle aside
as one might a fallen hair softly
from your face,
he channeled only Oprah
and stared instead at tax returns.

But a breeze outside beckoned.

1:04 a.m.

It was October air though April,
and he stumbled up steps,
beside the church, kitty-corner
from the sad old man
who beats his dogs; thinking
idly about things past,
places seen, and the corners of
the universe that only
a casual finger-snap from God
might redeem.

1:06 a.m.

A girl with a tattoo, stolen
away with the April rain,
pantomimes a marriage
in his mind.

Stalled,
he steps barefoot across
the asphalt, slicing
his way through the chill,
a desperate buoy floating
in an arctic fog.

1:08 a.m.

At the corner store he meets
a woman in a bathrobe; she
listens with him to the dumb growl
of a distant helicopter, to
thoughts careening like bumper cars,
to synapses firing blindly
about cat litter, love,
rentals and registrations;
about married women, monogamy,
misfortune and menstruation;
minstrels, alliterations,
dry erase boards,
beauty and skin-deep poetry,
about

playing pussies like a flute.

And the stars laughing
in the grim smoke of
her dying cigarette;
he remembers lies, hurt,
and recycles an erection,
sacrificing all naked things
for semen-bathed sheets
in a bed void otherwise of bodies,
she helps him home and
clutching a pillow
like a life preserver, falls in love.

She smells of pine,
cigarettes and perfume,
and Oprah in another room
chatters on about
premature ejaculations.

      1:19 a.m.

It was but nineteen minutes later,
and his life hadn't changed.

Praha, September 9th

Part of the human condition
is idling outside the pub
or singing in the shower.
It's watching someone you like
falling for someone you love.

It is inner thighs in your face,
pains in your back,
the world turning over
and over,
and over again
like a pinwheel,
a brutal and sexy oscillation.

It is the women
you pay to have sex with
and it is the women you don't.
It is sleeping with both of them,
afraid, wondering,
the smell of rubber from an ashtray,
the taste of ozone in your mouth,
the shame and bliss like the scent
of gasoline, or sweaty palms.

It is reading the words of dead men,
of knowing you're tracing tracks,
following the footsteps of a hundred
other fools before you.
It is the nausea and the libido.
It is beating off
thinking of them,
thinking of you,
thinking of what you've spent,
of what's been spent
nights and years and eons before.
It is losing your virginity once again
and for the last time.

Praha, August 22nd

The lightspeed of vaginas,
the flesh of sense.

Something in the beer boiled
and a woman ran her thigh
across your face. You
were silly, stupid
as she wore your glasses.
You were in love twice.

For one-hundred dollars
you could eat her soul, but
for free you could savor
the soft taste of guilt,
the watered down sex
rolling through your mouth
like ice cream,
like a spaceship,
like a cheap antidote swallowed
prior to its poison.

Neuchatel, Juillet 17th
"The Furry Tides of Lemmings"

I couldn't and didn't dare, they were
so peaceful fucking on the shore.

After his explosion they lay face-up
breathing hard and making tapestries with the stars.
I started to cry but grew tired.

When I awoke they were gone,
the seaside now saturated with dead hairy bodies.
I threw my clothes off and bathed beside them.

Lurid Illusion of Anger

He did not know it would make him dream of her,
of wetness, of longing, of her beautiful body
moving against his with the fury of the tides
of a thousand dead lemmings.

Scandalous

You kept peaking
at her inner thigh
when she sat cross-legged
like an Indian effigy
on your futon.

Wondering, you must,
what it might taste like
between your teeth, and
licking her from here to
eternity, what salivations,
what salvations
are stuck between baby-making hips
and might relieve you from
the harpsichord-like burdens of
this gravy-train, day-to-day, ashes-to-
ashes and dust-to- Norman-Rockwell-style
dust.

Jihlava, October 7th

Here at the end of the Velvet Revolution,
I remember a woman tossing her cigarette
down a storm drain.

We felt a kind of resolution yet regret
watching the cinders beneath the city
fade to black.

And then some thirteen years later
a little boy cries beside his mother.
He is wearing a Digimon sweater.

And we are thinking,
Mother, Father, this Earth is small.
I am between an ocean beside you.

Autumn

Her little cotton dress, her pink cotton dress
used to get caught in the winds of autumn.

We would all watch for glimpses,
of something heat-stroked and forbidden.

The blades of grass around her danced
like a cheap, beautiful Vegas strip number
and we threw our thoughtful dollars
at the stage, at her shoulders sun burned;
and sat soiling ourselves in pubescent rage.

With beards and older minds, we understand

soiling the beauty is half the beauty,
and in the midst of fall we were raised.

Neuchatel, Juillet 16th

this is sloppy love
bare-breasted hope on a European street
this is the crack peeling open your spine
the smile suspended, knees climbing
during the dance after you've asked
the smell of shame on her
hair you realize she agreed
courteously?
and so you swallow smile some
phlegm and a wad of ache

god, sometimes even still your heart
chasing every thigh that passes by

Neuchatel, Juillet 31st

At dinner we drink wines of silence.
The monk is missing, the brazen sage,
(you remember, yes, he hugged
even trees without reason) and Santé,
dear world, sailing courteously
through the furry tides of lemmings.
The trolls growing older, mother,
father, where is their childhood? Santé!
Dipping ourselves skinny and volatile,
our stupid naked bodies shake, skirmish
of our self-destructive bones.
And still no word from home.

Santé to strangers, to vast plains
of lonely rolling hills (you saw her
kicking the sheep, yodeling rumors),
mother, father, what is the nudity?
Why is the home? The handjobs?
I've a pair of panties in my heart,
and still no word from home.

Dear Mother and Father, Europe
opened its charred antiquity and
swallowed me. I digested for days.
This strange land, my feet in my hands,
my face an inflexible pear in the mirror, but
how old are the trolls now? The whiskey
is worse than wonderful; I am drunk, I am
drunk. On my way to eternity, drunk and
drunk – the pen is out of blood.

And still no word from home.

epilogue

Abandon

I smoke beautifully,
cigarette after cigarette,
lungs like charred cadavers caked with ash and frost
dangling somewhere in a freezer applaud this
miscalculation of self-control, this reckless misstep,
this brazen teeth-stained nicotine-crazed
misstep -- because they know, as smoke billows
from the butt of each dying cigarette, and passes
the panicking patrons waving away its great gray
cascade of beauty from their faces, it is
taking flight, hurling itself towards the clouds,
towards the moon, towards the great Big banging away
from us laughing, the indifferent rubber band
that gave us pools of proteins and polios and promises
of meaning.

And so,

I drink remarkably, too,
whiskey after whiskey after scotch after ale
like a liver attached to a teat suckling away
the drunken abuses of an unforgiving mother;
sweet sand-woven grooves this liver leaves like
the footsteps of a snake slithering through the baked dunes;
downtrodden, mistaken roadkill sizzling
somewhere on the Interstates outside Mesquite
where landscapes evaporate in thick strings of heat,
parading anyhow the horizon as a slick drunken blur,
stumbling vertically towards the clouds where
marshmallow gods, those infinite infants, bask in
the radiant glow of our mistakes, smoking rays
of ozone, drinking our despairs, and huffing whatever
afflictions and addictions we send their way.

Why all this talk of air?
Because we are the cold, the broken, the abused,
the aching, the pressed, the weary, the used,
the wanton, the willful, the cornered, the crossed,
the wasted, the dreaming, the sleep-walking stumbling,
fumbling, insomniatic tumbling, the
crazy crass sea animal living, loving, looking
addicted to the sky, wanting
to fly in that air –

that cruel quadrillion tons of mass weighing down
on us, on you, and me, and teasing
with that sly indifference, that god-like godlessness,
that undisclosed and vague balance
between evolutionary science and
intelligently designed nonsense.

And so, I drink coffee;
because it mixes well with Bacardi,
because the sexy sting of cigarette smoke after a sip
is itself a self-defined and charcoal-colored skinny dip
into that eternal pool of proteins and prayers,
where our hopes collide and our dreams despair:
the sweet silly thoughts of an afterlife.

www.ingramcontent.com/pod-product-compliance
Lightning Source LLC
La Vergne TN
LVHW011241080426
835509LV00005B/584